Penguins

Published by Wildlife Education, Ltd.
12233 Thatcher Court, Poway, California 92064
contact us at: 1-800-477-5034
e-mail at: animals@zoobooks.com
visit us at: www.zoobooks.com

ISBN 1-888153-30-X

Penguins

Created and Written by
John Bonnett Wexo

Zoological Consultant
Charles R. Schroeder, D.V.M.
Director Emeritus
San Diego Zoo &
San Diego Wild Animal Park

Scientific Consultants
George Gaylord Simpson, Ph.D.
The Simroe Foundation

Bernard Stonehouse, Ph.D.
Scott Polar Research Institute
Cambridge

Frank S. Todd
Corporate Curator of Birds
Sea World, Inc.

Contents

Penguins are high on the list of animals that people love the most. And it's easy to see why. Penguins sometimes look like funny little people. They stand on their legs like people and waddle around. They often hold their wings down at their sides like human arms. And their feathers sometimes look like the black-and-white formal suits that people wear at weddings.

Penguins also seem to *like* people, or at least not to mind them. Unlike most other wild animals, penguins don't usually run away when a human approaches. Instead, they may walk right up to a human and look him or her right in the eye. They seem to be saying, "How do you do, and how are you?"

Beyond all this, penguins are simply beautiful animals that are interesting to watch. Their feathers are sleek and shiny. And many have handsome patterns or colorful feathers on their heads that make them look very splendid indeed.

Male and female penguins of each species look very much the same. The patterns and colors on their bodies look alike. The males may be a little larger than the females, and their beaks may be a little bigger. But it's very hard to tell a male from a female just by looking at them.

As everybody knows, penguins cannot fly. In fact, the various kinds of penguins make up the largest family of flightless birds in the world. There are at least 18 different kinds of penguins, and the total number of penguins on earth is probably very large. Some people believe that there may be more than *100 million penguins* living today.

Nobody is really sure how long penguins can live. One penguin in a zoo lived more than 30 years. But penguins outside of zoos probably don't live nearly that long.

As the map at the right shows, all penguins live in the southern half of the earth—the Southern Hemisphere. There are no penguins in the Northern Hemisphere.

Many people are surprised to learn that penguins do not always live in cold places. As the map shows, there is one penguin species that lives right on the Equator, where it can get hot. Other penguins live in places where it is warm at least part of the year. For instance, there are penguins along the coast of South America. And there are penguins living in southern Australia, South Africa, and New Zealand.

Some penguins live on islands inside the Antarctic Circle during the summer, but migrate to warmer places to spend the winter. They may swim thousands of miles. Only two species of penguins (Adelies and Emperors) live in very cold areas all year long.

EQUATOR

SOUTH AMERICA

AFRICA

● SOUTH POLE

ANTARCTICA

NEW ZEALAND

AUSTRALIA

Orange areas are places penguins live.

GENTOO PENG

There's a lot of **variety** in the penguin family. Many people think that all penguins look alike, but nothing could be further from the truth. Every species has its own unique markings and colors. And penguins come in many different sizes.

The largest are the Emperor penguins, and the smallest are the Little Blue penguins. (See if you can find them in the picture.) A full-grown Emperor can stand almost 3½ feet tall. And it can weigh more than 90 pounds. Little Blue penguins are only about 16 inches tall. And they weigh less than 2½ pounds.

SNARES CRESTED PENGUIN
Eudyptes robustus

EMPEROR PENGUIN
Aptenodytes forsteri

ROCKHOPPER PENGUIN
Eudyptes crestatus

ERECT-CRESTED PENGUIN
Eudyptes atratus

BLACKFOOTED PENGUIN
Spheniscus demersus

ADELIE PENGUIN
Pygoscelis adeliae

FIORDLAND CRESTED PENGUIN
Eudyptes Pachyrhynchus

YELLOW-EYED PENGUIN
Megadyptes antipodes

CHINSTRAP PENGUIN
Pygoscelis antarctica

KING PENGUIN
Aptenodytes patagonica

MACARONI PENGUIN
Eudyptes chrysolophus

ROYAL PENGUIN
Eudyptes schlegeli

GENTOO PENGUIN
Pygoscelis papua

MAGELLANIC PENGUIN
Spheniscus magellanicus

WHITE-FLIPPERED PENGUIN
Eudyptula albosignata

PERUVIAN PENGUIN
Spheniscus humboldti

GALAPAGOS PENGUIN
Spheniscus mendiculus

LITTLE BLUE PENGUIN
Eudyptula minor

9

The body of a penguin is made for swimming in the ocean and catching food underwater. Most penguins can swim faster and dive deeper than any other birds.

On these pages, you will see that there is a direct connection between the wonderful swimming abilities of penguins and the fact that they cannot fly. In order to swim very well, penguins had to give up some of the things that make it possible for other birds to fly. For example, penguins actually *need* wings that are *too small for flying*. And they need bodies that are too heavy for flight, as shown below.

Flying birds need large wings to hold them up in the air. But small wings are better for birds that swim.

SEE FOR YOURSELF why the heavy body of a penguin is better for swimming and diving than the light body of a flying bird. Put two containers in water. Leave one container empty and put some sand into the second container. The body of a penguin is like the second container. It is heavier and sinks lower in the water.

Now push down slowly on both containers, using equal force. As you gradually increase the force on both, you will see that the sand-filled container is easier to push down in the water. In the same way, it is easier for a penguin to dive than it is for a lighter bird. And it is easier for a penguin to stay underwater, too.

The bodies of penguins are shaped like submarines. This streamlining helps them to cut through the water with ease.

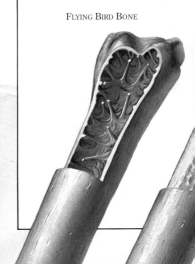

FLYING BIRD BONE

Light birds, like the duck above, float high in the water. They can only use their feet to push them when they swim. Heavier penguins float lower, and can use their powerful wings to push them. This is one reason why penguins can swim much faster.

Large wings are clumsy in water. The long feathers on the wings bend and drag through the water. And this cuts down the swimming power of the wings. The small wings of penguins are stiff like paddles, and they are covered with very small feathers. They push water better and provide more swimming power.

SEE FOR YOURSELF how a small wing is best for swimming. First, try to paddle water with a large sheet of paper **①**. Like the large wing of a flying bird, the paper flops over and doesn't push water very well. Next, fold another sheet of paper five or six times and try paddling with it **②**. The smaller and stiffer paper pushes better, like a penguin's wing.

FLYING BIRD WING

PENGUIN WING

Penguin feathers are very small and tightly packed. There are more than 70 feathers per square inch. The feathers overlap and are coated with oil, and this makes them waterproof.

A penguin's wings work like two paddles. They swing back and forth to drive the penguin through the water. Like paddles, the wings are very stiff. They have large flat bones inside them to keep them from bending.

The muscles that move the wings are very strong. They are the largest muscles in a penguin's body.

PENGUIN BONE

Flying birds often have hollow bones that are filled with air. This helps to reduce the weight of their bodies and makes it easier for them to get off the ground. But penguins have solid, heavy bones. This helps to increase the weight of their bodies and makes it easier for them to swim and dive.

The large body of a penguin has plenty of room inside for holding food. Emperor penguins, like the one above, may eat 30 pounds of food at one time.

Penguins are at home in the ocean. They spend most of their time in the water, looking for food. And they seem to feel much more comfortable in water than they do on land.

Some penguins stay close to the shore and never swim too far from their breeding colonies. They fish during the day and come back to the shore every night. Other species may take long journeys across the open ocean. They even sleep in the water. Some kinds of crested penguins may stay at sea for five months or more. They may swim thousands of miles, and never come within sight of land the whole time.

Penguins are wonderful long-distance swimmers. They often travel in large groups. As they swim, they pop out of the water to gulp air and then plunge back in again. By doing this, they can get the air they need without slowing down. This kind of swimming is called "porpoising" because porpoises sometimes swim in a similar way.

Like all animals, penguins need water to drink. But when they are at sea, the only water they can get is salt water. For this reason, they have special glands that remove salt from the water they drink. The salt is removed in a liquid form. It flows down grooves in a penguin's beak and drips off the end.

The black-and-white "suit" of a penguin is more than just cute. It helps to hide the penguin from predators when it is swimming in the ocean. When a penguin is swimming near the surface, its white underside makes it hard for Leopard seals or other predators below the penguin to see it.

The white underside of the penguin blends with the bright light coming from above, as shown at right.

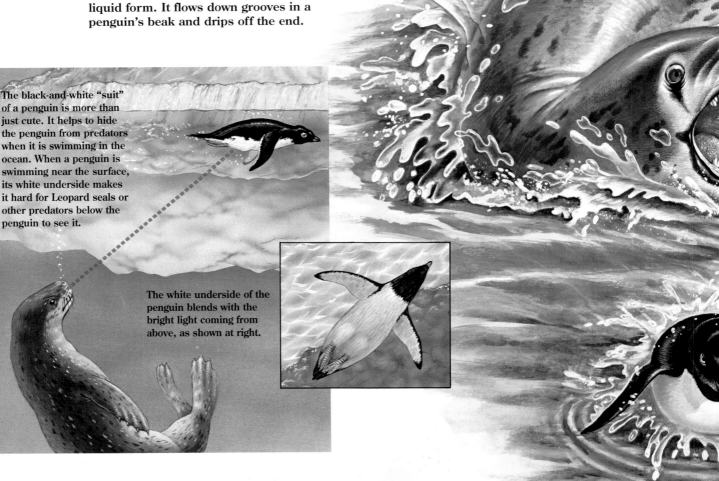

The normal swimming speed of most penguins is about 15 miles per hour. This is equal to the speed of the fastest human runner and *four times faster* than the fastest human swimmer. Penguins swim about as fast as the bottlenose dolphins that many people have seen streaking around pools at oceanariums.

Penguins get all of their food from the sea. They dive to catch fish, squid, and small shrimp-like animals called *krill*. When they have a choice, each kind of penguin seems to prefer one kind of food. For example, Adelie penguins like krill, and Blackfooted penguins like fish. But if they can't get their favorite food, all penguins will usually eat whatever happens to be available.

KRILL

FISH

SQUID

The favorite foods of penguins are found at different depths in the ocean. So different kinds of penguins usually dive to different depths to find the food they like best. Adelies stay close to the surface, where krill is plentiful. Some crested penguins dive deeper to find fish. And Emperor penguins may dive almost *900 feet down* to catch large squid. Emperors dive deeper than any other bird.

The ocean can be a dangerous place for penguins. Many predators in the sea hunt penguins, including sea lions, fur seals, and killer whales. The most dangerous predator of all is probably the Leopard seal. Leopard seals like the one above may eat more than 15 Adelie penguins *a day*. But they usually catch only weak or sick penguins. A healthy penguin can often swim faster than a Leopard seal and get away.

ADELIE PENGUINS

The penguins here are probably well aware of the hungry seal swimming nearby. Chances are they will wait until the seal has gone before jumping into the ocean to hunt or play.

15

On land, penguins are not as comfortable as they are in water. In fact, if they had a choice about it, most penguins would probably never come out of the water. But they don't have a choice. They must come ashore for at least part of every year to have babies and grow new feathers. These things cannot be done in the ocean.

Life on land presents some problems that penguins do not have in water. Often, they must survive in very cold weather. And of course, they must be able to walk.

Adelie and Emperor penguins can stay alive in colder weather than any other animals on earth. Of all the penguins, they have the best systems for controlling their body temperatures. An Adelie can actually be buried up to its neck in snow and still be as warm inside its body as a penguin that lives on the Equator.

Like humans, penguins are *warm-blooded*. They make heat inside their bodies. And this means they can stay warm if they can keep most of this heat from leaving their bodies. To keep the heat from escaping, their bodies have several layers of insulation. On the outside, there are tightly packed feathers. Under that, there is a layer of air. Then the skin, and under the skin a thick layer of fat called *blubber*. The layers of insulation are like the layers of clothing you put on when you want to keep warm.

The wonderful insulation of penguins makes it possible for them to live in very cold places. But it can cause problems when the weather turns warmer—as it sometimes does even in Antarctica. Then, penguins must have ways to *let heat out* of their bodies, or they might fry inside their own skins. One of the best ways that penguins use for getting rid of heat is shown below:

1

3

When a penguin's feathers are held tight against the body **(1)**, they help to keep body heat in—like a door helps to keep heat inside a hot room **(2)**.

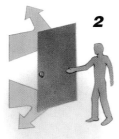

2

But penguins can fluff up their feathers, so the heat can escape between the raised feathers **(3)**. This is like opening the door **(4)**.

4

FLYING BIRD

PENGUIN

Penguins stand up straight like people because their legs are attached to their bodies at one end. An upright posture is the only way they can balance their bodies over their legs. If penguins leaned forward like other birds, they would fall on their faces.

1

SEE FOR YOURSELF why penguins cannot walk like other birds. Take a ruler and pretend that it is the body of a bird. First, balance the ruler by placing your finger in the middle①. This is the way most birds balance their bodies when walking, because their legs are near the center of their bodies. Next, balance the ruler by placing your finger at the end②. This is the way penguins must balance, because their legs are at one end of their bodies.

2

When there is snow on the ground, penguins have a way of moving fast on land. They just fall on their stomachs and slide like little sleds. To keep moving, they push with their wings and feet, like a skier using poles. This is called *tobogganing* (tuh-bog-uhn-ing). Penguins can toboggan for many miles.

To get ashore, most penguins just swim up to a beach and walk the rest of the way. But Adelie penguins have a spectacular way of getting out of the water. They swim very fast under the water and then shoot up in the air like little rockets. They can pop straight up into the air a distance of six feet or more. Because Adelies are only about two feet tall, that means they can jump three times their own height. For a human swimmer to match this, he or she would have to jump 18 feet out of the water.

Most people think that all penguins walk the same way, by waddling slowly along. But each penguin species has its own way of walking. Gentoo penguins trot briskly. Emperor penguins sway from side to side. And Rockhoppers live up to their name by hopping from rock to rock, as shown above. Rockhoppers sometimes jump six feet in a single hop.

On land, most penguins live in large colonies called rookeries. Some of the largest rookeries have over one million penguins in them. Penguins chatter and fight a lot in a rookery, so the noise can be louder than a crowd at a football game.

KING PENGUINS

Baby penguins come into this world like all other birds. They hatch from eggs. Obviously, bird eggs cannot be laid or hatched in the middle of the ocean, so adult penguins must come ashore each year to have their babies.

Most penguins build nests and lay their eggs in them. Like other birds, they sit on the eggs and warm them until they hatch. And like other birds, penguin parents spend most of their time getting food for the young chicks after they hatch. Most penguin females have two chicks a year, although three eggs are sometimes laid.

As you will see below, King penguins and Emperor penguins do things differently.

Most penguins come back to the same place every year to have their babies. Some of them may swim thousands of miles to get there. Like human sailors, they probably use the sun to guide them.

The males usually get to the nest area first. When the females arrive a few days later, both partners greet each other with a little ceremony. Adelie penguins usually raise their beaks in the air and spread their wings to say "hello."

Emperor and King penguins don't build nests. Instead, they carry their eggs around *on their feet*. After the eggs hatch, the mothers and fathers take turns carrying the baby penguins around on their feet. When it gets cold, both eggs and chicks can be covered with a flap of skin that keeps them warm.

Emperor penguin chicks would quickly freeze if their parents did not help to keep them warm.

Small bodies cool faster than big bodies, because they cannot hold heat as well. You can see this when you blow on hot cereal to cool it off. It is much easier to cool a small teaspoon of cereal than it is to cool a big bowl of it.

There are many different kinds of penguin nests. Some penguins that live in warmer places like to make their nests in holes in the ground. The chicks are very safe from predators in these nests.

In the coldest places, there are no plants. So penguins just gather some rocks together for a nest.

When nests are built on top of the ground, they may be made of all sorts of materials. It really depends on what the penguins can find. If there is grass in the area, this will be used. And penguins sometimes use sticks, seaweed, feathers, or moss.

The babies of Emperor penguins are hatched in the worst weather on earth. Female Emperors lay their eggs during the coldest months of the Antarctic winter. Then the males balance the eggs on their feet and keep them warm for six very cold weeks. The males huddle together for warmth. Blizzard winds of 120 miles per hour may blow, and the temperature may drop to *80 degrees below zero* (Fahrenheit).

Baby penguins are hungry all the time. Their parents must make many trips to the ocean each day to catch enough fish to feed them. At times, the parents may feed their chicks two pounds of food *per hour*.

When they first hatch, baby penguins are covered with soft, downy feathers ①. At about six weeks of age, Adelie penguins start to molt, or shed these feathers ②.

By the time Adelie chicks are eight weeks old, they have shed their baby down. They now look very much like adult Adelies, except that the feathers under their chins are white ③.

The young Adelies grow very fast. By the time they are only two months old, they are large enough to go to sea.

21

The future of penguins looks good, when you first look at it. After all, there are millions of penguins alive today. And most of them live in remote areas where people seldom bother them. Nobody hunts or traps penguins. Nobody makes coats out of their skins or carvings out of their beaks. In fact, all penguin species are totally protected by law.

If any animals are safe from extinction, it certainly should be penguins. But scientists are finding that even penguins cannot escape completely from some of the things that people are doing to the earth. Nobody is trying to hurt penguins, but we may be hurting them anyway.

The problem has to do with the ocean. Penguins depend completely on the ocean for life. They get all of their food from it and they spend most of their lives swimming in it. The millions of penguins alive today need millions of tons of fish, squid, and krill to stay alive every year.

As the human population continues to grow, people are taking more and more food from areas of the oceans where penguins feed. In some places, people have taken so much fish from the sea that there may not be enough food to keep large numbers of penguins alive. Off the west coast of South America, for example, people take billions of anchovies from the sea every year.